DR. MARTIN
LUTHER KING, JR.

DR. MARTIN LUTHER KING, JR.

BY GLORIA D. MIKLOWITZ

tempo
books

GROSSET & DUNLAP, INC.
A FILMWAYS COMPANY
Publishers New York

For Helen H. Jones with admiration and affection.

PICTURE CREDITS:
Cover: Freelance Photographers' Guild
Wide World: all other photos.

CONTENTS

CHAPTER ONE

ROOTS

Dr. Martin Luther King, Jr. was a fighter for people's rights. He believed in *nonviolence*—peaceful ways to win change. Instead of fists or guns, he fought with words and reason. Because of his efforts, many laws, unfair to black people, were changed. The problems of the poor became important to the entire nation. Americans of every color began to understand and accept each other better.

Dr. King was killed by an assassin's bullet on April 4, 1968. In July, 1977, his widow, Coretta King, went to Washington, D.C. There, she accepted the Medal of Freedom for her dead husband. It is the country's highest civilian award. When he made the presentation, President Jimmy Carter said, "We know that he lives now and will live a thousand years from now in the hearts and minds of men."

*   *   *

One day, when Martin Luther King, Jr. was a child, his father took him to buy a pair of shoes. Reverend King led Martin to a seat near the front of the shoe store. A clerk came up and said, "Move to the rear of the store, please. I'll serve you there."

Rev. King felt that just being black was no reason to move. After all, he was an important and respected man in the city of Atlanta, Georgia. He was head of the Ebenezer Baptist Church. For 37 years his wife's father had headed the same church. He was president of the National Association for the Advancement of Colored People (NAACP).

So, Rev. King did not move. Instead, he said to the clerk that the benches in the back of the store were no more comfortable than those in the front. And, he added, he expected that the shoes the clerk might bring would be the same, wherever he sat. So, he would stay where he was.

"Blacks sit in the back, or they don't get served," the clerk said. "It's the law!" Rev. King got up, took Martin's hand, and left the store.

Only a few years ago many southern states had laws unfair to black people. They could not eat in restaurants where white people ate. They could not go to schools where white

Southern states had separate public waiting rooms
for blacks. Schools, buses and restaurants were also
segregated.

children studied. They could not use the same public rest rooms or drink from the same water fountains. It was against the law to sit next to white people in movies or on trains and buses. If seats reserved for whites filled up, a black had to give up his or her seat. These unfair laws were called *Jim Crow laws*.

The King family did not like the Jim Crow laws, but they could do nothing about them. They were well off, but that did not protect them from injustice. They lived in a two-story wood home in a part of Atlanta where the successful black people lived.

Once, when Martin was in a car with his father, a policeman asked Rev. King to pull over. "Listen, *boy*!" the officer began, coming to the window. Rev. King's voice was cold. He pointed to Martin. "*That* is a boy," he said. "*I* am a man."

Martin and his younger brother Alfred Daniel, called A.D., shared a bike. They had a white friend who loved to ride on the handlebars. For some time the three children were good friends. But one day the white boy's mother came to Martin's house. Martin was not to play with her son anymore, she said.

Why, Martin wanted to know. His mother and grandmother tried to explain. They said it was because the Kings were black. White people did not like their children to play with black children. Then they explained how black Africans first came to America as slaves. But after the Civil War, black people were given their freedom by law. Although blacks should have the same rights as whites, according to the Constitution, it didn't work that way. Many people still treated blacks as if they were still slaves. In Atlanta, the

The problems of his people worried Martin even as
a child. Here, years later, he listens as a mother tell
of her children's need for shoes.

whites controlled the businesses. They said black people were ignorant and should "know their place."

Rev. King tried to ease Martin's hurt. "Remember this," he said often. "You are as good as anybody else!"

Learning was very important in the King home. Mrs. King, who had been a school teacher, taught the children to read before they were of school age. Martin learned quickly. When he started school, he was so good at reading that they put him into second grade with his older sister Christine.

As soon as Martin could read well, he read everything he could find about his people. He bought books about slavery and about the Civil War. He learned about Nat Turner, the slave who rose up against his masters, and Frederick Douglass, the slave who became a great statesman.

It made him proud of being black.

By the time he was thirteen, he figured that to make it in a white world, a black man had to do two things. He had to be twice as good a person as a white. And he had to be twice as smart as everyone else.

In high school, Martin was active on a debating team. One day, his team went to a nearby city for a competition. Martin did not do well. On the way home in the bus, he and the other black students were told to go to the back of the bus. Martin just looked out the window. The driver came up to him and said, "Hey, I mean you! Get out of that seat and let those people sit down." When Martin and a friend didn't move, the driver turned ugly. "Nigger," he said, "I'm going to call the police. We'll see if you'll move."

His teacher, Miss Sara Grace Bradley, came to Martin's side. She spoke quietly to him, begging him to move for her sake. Slowly, Martin got up. Finding no seats in the rear of the bus, he stood for nearly two hours, hanging onto a strap. It was hard being a good person when the laws treated you unfairly and when white people didn't practice what they preached.

Because he was such a good student, Martin skipped the seventh and twelfth grades. He graduated from high school at 15 and was accepted as a freshman at Morehouse College. The college was in Atlanta, so he could live at home. It was the same school his father had graduated from. There he would study English and social studies.

He hungered for learning. Words were delicious to him. Ideas were more fun than sports. While other students relaxed after hours on the ball field, Martin relaxed in the col-

In 1948, Martin was attending Morehouse College.

lege library. He read hundreds of books on American and black history. Late at night he liked to play with his new knowledge, tossing words and ideas back and forth with friends just as others tossed balls.

Still, Martin was not the best student. In his first year, he got a C in philosophy. He was slow to turn in papers. He was more interested in dressing well and going out with pretty girls.

For a while, Martin wasn't sure what career he wanted to follow. His mother wanted him to be a doctor. He thought maybe he would be a lawyer. His father hoped he would become a minister and share the pulpit with him. Martin wanted to please his father, but he wasn't sure.

Food and the church were the two most important things to many southern blacks. The church was the only place they could escape from their worries. On Sundays, black churches were crowded. But most black preachers used the church to whip up the emotions of the people, not to solve their problems. There was a lot of hand-clapping and "amen-shouting." Martin felt the church should be used to get ideas to people, a place to give direction and help.

In his senior year at Morehouse, Martin finally decided. He would be a preacher. Maybe he could make the people think and talk of progress *after* they left the church.

Rev. King was very pleased. He suggested Martin give a trial church service in a small room of his big church. Then if Martin didn't do well, there would be no shame. But, as word spread that a 17-year-old would preach, many said they would come. The service had to be moved to the main church. Martin stood before the big congregation for the first time. In his deep, sincere voice, he preached about human suffering.

The next year he was ordained a minister. Though he was only 18, he become the assistant pastor of Ebenezer Baptist Church, his father's church.

Rev. King, Sr. wanted his son to come home after college. But Martin had other plans. At 19, with a degree from Morehouse College, he enrolled at Crozer Theological Seminary in Chester, Pennsylvania. There, he would go on to study for the master's degree in philosophy.

CHAPTER TWO

MOVING ON

Crozer Seminary was in the North. Martin liked that. In the North he could sit anywhere he wanted in a restaurant or theater. There he was treated as an equal. Going to school in the North had another advantage. He would be away from "Daddy" King who expected Martin to follow in his footsteps. Martin wanted to be his own man, make up his own mind.

There were only six black students among 94 whites at Crozer. Martin's color didn't matter. Because he was first in his class and was well liked, he was elected president of the student body.

During the year at Crozer, Martin went to hear the president of Howard University lecture on his trip to India. It was a turning point in his life. From Dr. Mordicai Johnson he learned about Mahatma Gandhi, the Indian leader who brought about change for his people through non-violence.

Gandhi aroused the people of his country to free themselves from British rule. He forbade his followers to raise a hand against the British or to fire a shot. Gandhi was jailed often, but he never fought back. In jail, he protested the wrongs done to him and his people by going without food for long periods of time. Once,

Gandhi and his followers walked hundreds of miles to the sea to make their own salt. They were protesting a British tax on salt. Change came to India slowly, but it came. Gandhi's nonviolence toward his enemies brought about the change.

The idea that social change could be brought about by peaceful means, through love, excited Martin. Later, it would become the philosophy he used to bring about change in America.

By December, 1951, Martin had changed schools again. This time he moved to Boston College in Massachusetts. There he began work on a doctoral degree. His small apartment became the meeting place of black students. They drank coffee together and talked for hours about politics and the way the poor and blacks were treated. Black men had fought and died for their country during

This picture, taken seven years after Martin became pastor of the Dexter Avenue Baptist Church, shows Martin Luther King, III, Martin, Coretta, Dexter Scott, and Yoki (Yolanda).

World War II. But now that the war was over, they were still treated as second-class citizens.

Around Christmas time, Martin's father wrote about his coming home to "settle down." There was a girl waiting for him, but Martin wasn't interested. He had outgrown his childhood sweetheart.

Martin often missed the South, especially the good soul food— hog jowls, chitterlings and collard greens. He also missed southern girls. A married friend offered to introduce him to a pretty girl from Alabama who was studying music in Boston. Coretta Scott was a nice girl, intelligent and independent, the friend said. She had medium-dark skin, large bright eyes and a natural singing voice. Coretta wanted to become a concert singer. She also wanted to stay in the North, where she would be accepted as equal with whites.

Coming from Alabama, Coretta had seen her father's home and business burned because he was an "uppity" black man. She didn't want to return to a South where blacks were treated that way.

Martin liked Coretta immediately. But she didn't like him at first. She thought he was not too well trained, was too pious and narrow-minded. Still, they began seeing each other.

Before she would marry Martin, he had to agree that she could go back to Boston to finish her studies. Martin wanted to complete his doctoral degree, too. But Coretta also wanted him to promise he'd take a job in the North. To that he would say only, "We'll see."

They were married on June 18, 1953 at the bride's home. Everybody who was anybody in black social life was at the big wedding. Soon after, Coretta and Martin returned to Boston to finish their schooling.

Martin began receiving job offers in the North. A church in Boston and one in New York wanted him as their pastor. Offers of a teaching position and a job as dean came from northern colleges. Coretta hoped he would accept one of these. But Martin wanted to return to the South. "Daddy" King urged him to come to Atlanta and share the pulpit at his church.

Then an offer came from the Dexter Avenue Baptist Church in Montgomery, Alabama. Martin had spoken to the congregation of mostly doctors, lawyers and professors. He liked the people there. They would want a preacher with ideas, not one who led them in foot-stomping and amen-shouting.

So when the job was offered, Martin accepted it. He asked only that they let him go back to Boston until he and Coretta could finish their schooling.

In January, 1954, Coretta and Martin stood across the street from the church that was to be Martin's first parish. It was a plain, red-brick building with a small, white steeple. Inside, sun filtered through stained glass windows to the polished old wood pews. Martin vowed he would be a new kind of preacher. His church would be a place where God was worshipped, but also where ideas could be shared.

He would expect his people to be good Christians *every* day of the week, not just Sunday. He wanted them all to join the NAACP. Only 2,000 of the 50,000 blacks in Montgomery were registered to vote. He asked everyone over the age of 21 to go out and register.

Ten years after he took his first job, Martin was respected all over the world. Here he is shown with
Senator Edward Kennedy.

Soon after arriving in Montgomery, Martin met the Reverend Ralph David Abernathy. Rev. Abernathy was pastor of the First Baptist Church. They were to become very close friends.

Martin learned a lot about how things were in Montgomery from Rev. Abernathy. Most of the blacks worked as servants. Nearby were two air bases where many blacks worked. Only at the bases were blacks and whites treated equally.

Some months before his arrival, the Supreme Court, the highest court in the country, had made a ruling. It made separate schools for blacks and whites illegal. The whites of Montgomery and other parts of the South were angry at the ruling. They would either ignore it or work around it. They had no intention of allowing black children to study with theirs. In fact, they had no in-

Only six years after he went to Montgomery, he was awarded an honorary degree by Lincoln University in Oxford, Pennsylvania.

tention of changing any of the old rules. They felt that blacks needed to know their place.

Martin settled into his new job quickly. He would wake at 5A.M. and work for three hours on his sermon. During the day he would perform marriages, visit sick or dying church members and go to meetings or luncheons. He soon realized that the black leaders of Montgomery were divided. Instead of working together when a race problem came up, they competed with each other. Each one wanted power. If the blacks of Montgomery were divided, how could they fight segregation?

What was needed, everyone agreed, was a cause that would bring them all together. It was Rosa Parks who created that cause. Her act started Martin Luther King, Jr. on the crusade which was to absorb the rest of his life.

CHAPTER THREE

IT ALL BEGAN WITH ROSA PARKS

It was a mean, windy evening in Montgomery, Alabama on December 1, 1955. It was mostly blacks who waited at the bus stops along Cleveland Avenue. Tired from their day's work or from shopping, they looked forward to getting home.

Rosa Parks, a middle-aged seamstress, was one of those blacks. A thin woman who loved to read, she was dressed neatly and wore rimless glasses. Most of the day she had spent bent over, pinning hems and marking seams of white women's dresses. Later she had gone Christmas shopping. Now her back ached and her legs hurt. She could hardly wait to get on the bus and sit down.

When the bus stopped, Mrs. Parks followed the rules for blacks. She waited her turn to get on and pay her fare. Then she rushed back down the two front steps and hurried with other blacks to the rear door. She hoped the driver wouldn't close that door before she had a chance to get on.

Finally Mrs. Parks found a seat in the fifth row, on the left. The first four rows were for whites only. As the bus moved into traffic, she relaxed. How good it was to sit and stare out the window at the passing streets.

In the next minutes, the bus

stopped again and again. More blacks and some whites got on. Soon all the seats in the first four rows were filled with whites. Rosa Parks didn't notice. She was tired and her mind was elsewhere.

"All right, all right," the driver said when he saw whites standing. "Come on. Get in the back," he told Mrs. Parks and two other blacks.

Rosa Parks looked up at the strong white man waiting for her seat and didn't move.

"Get out of that seat," the driver said, pointing at her.

"No," she said. "I won't."

The bus became as silent as a church. The driver had to do something, or lose face. He pulled to a stop and went for help.

When the driver came back, a policeman was with him. The officer lifted Mrs. Parks under the arms. "What did I do against the law?"

Rosa Parks being fingerprinted.

shc asked. He didn't answer. She was charged with disobeying race laws on publicly owned buses.

Within an hour, the news of Mrs. Parks' arrest spread. Blacks phoned their friends and pastors. Mrs. Parks, allowed one phone call, reached E. D. Nixon. She had been his secretary when he was president of the local NAACP. Nixon phoned the police and asked what the charge was. "None of your . . . business," an officer said. And he hung up.

Now Mrs. Jo Ann Robinson, president of the Women's Political Council entered the story. For months she had been looking for a way to attack the unfair seating rules of the Montgomery bus lines. Rosa Parks, respectable, soft-spoken, had been arrested because of those unfair rules. She was the perfect case to fight the injustice.

When Mrs. Parks was bailed out of jail, she was asked if she would be willing to fight the charge. Nixon said she would lose her job and probably not get work anywhere in Montgomery if she agreed to fight. Mrs. Parks said that didn't matter.

Nixon and Robinson believed that the only way to fight back was through the white pocketbook. If the blacks stopped riding the buses, *boycotted* them, the bus company would lose money. If they lost too much money, they would have to change the rules or go out of business.

Nixon made phone calls all through the night. He was trying to get the help of all Montgomery's black leaders. Early on Friday, December 2, he reached Martin. He asked if Martin would be a member of a committee for a one-day boycott. Martin wanted time to think it over.

He called his friend Ralph Abernathy for advice. Rev. Abernathy sensed the importance of the boycott even more than Martin. "Join," he urged.

The first meeting to decide what to do was held at Martin's church. Over 40 important black men and women showed up. All, even the ministers who usually differed, agreed. It was time to act, not just talk. A bus boycott was decided on. The bus company must be made to show respect to black passengers.

The boycott was set for Monday, December 5, four days after the Parks incident. Sheets were printed up. One read:

1. *Don't ride the bus to work, to town, to school, or any place Monday, December 5.*

2. *Another Negro woman has been arrested and put in jail*

because she refused to give up her bus seat.

3. *Don't ride the bus to work, to town, to school, or anywhere on Monday. If you work, take a cab, share a ride or walk.*

4. *Come to a mass meeting Monday at 7 P.M. at the Holt Street Baptist Church for further instructions.*

When school let out Friday, black children began passing out announcements to their people all over the city. One such paper was given to a black cleaning lady. She couldn't read. She asked her employer to read it to her. The employer was shocked. She read it to the editor of the local newspaper. On Sunday, the newspaper published the boycott announcement on its front page. It enraged the white people of the city. But it also publicized the event. Now almost all blacks in the city knew about the boycott called for the next day.

Though few realized it, history was being made in Montgomery. If the blacks could unite in the boycott, it would show they had tremendous power.

All day Sunday, pastors in the black churches spoke of the Monday boycott. Now the question was—would it work?

At 5:30A.M. Monday, Martin and Coretta King were up and dressed. It was still dark outside. The first bus, which stopped a few feet from the King home, was due at 6A.M. Coretta fed Yolanda, nicknamed Yoki, their first child. Both Martin and Coretta worried that the boycott might not work.

At 6A.M., Coretta looked out the living room window. "Martin! Martin! Come quickly!" she called. He rushed to her side to see the first bus moving away. It was empty!

They could hardly believe it. This bus normally carried more blacks to and from work than any other. The Kings stood at the window waiting for the next bus, fifteen minutes later. It, too, was empty. The third bus came and went. It held two passengers, both white!

Martin was overjoyed. It didn't seem possible that a protest, organized over only one weekend, could work so well. He jumped into his car and checked around the city. He counted only eight blacks on buses at the height of the morning rush.

Blacks, boycotting the buses, thumbed rides to school or walked. Some rode mules to their work. Some had cars and drove around picking up walking blacks. Taxis were full.

In February, 1956, Martin was booked by police. With him is his friend Reverend Ralph David Abernathy.

Meanwhile, Rosa Parks' case came to trial. She was charged with disobeying a law on purpose, then refusing to correct the wrong when asked to. The judge fined her ten dollars, and "four dollars cost of court."

Monday afternoon, black ministers and other black leaders held a meeting. They voted to keep the boycott going. Each day the boycott went on would hurt white bank accounts.

At that meeting Martin was asked to be president of a group to be called the Montgomery Improvement Association (MIA). He was stunned and delighted.

That night, Martin stood before a packed audience at the Holt Street Church. Loudspeakers carried his words to 4,000 more people jamming the streets.

Martin told what had happened to Rosa Parks. "There comes a time," he said, wagging an angry finger, "when people get tired . . . tired of being segregated and humiliated, tired of being kicked about..." Black patience was wearing thin, he said. Only freedom and justice would sattisfy blacks now. Freedom and justice would be brought about, but not through violence, which was the way of the whites.

"If you will protest courageously, and with dignity and Christian love," he said, "when the history books are written, the historians will say: There lived a great people, a black people—who injected new meaning and dignity into the veins of civilization."

Martin's speech brought everyone to his feet. The shouts and whistles and roars of the crowd shook the church. In that moment, Martin Luther King, Jr. raised the battle cry of nonviolence. Adopting Gandhi's way of protest, he was calling on all blacks to unite for a long struggle. What blacks wanted, through peaceful protest, were their civil rights. And they wanted them Now.

CHAPTER FOUR

PEACEFUL PROTEST IN MONTGOMERY

Blacks wanted nothing more than what whites already enjoyed. They wanted polite treatment from bus drivers. They wanted to be seated on a first come, first served basis, and they were even willing to sit in the back if that's the way the bus filled up. They wanted black drivers for routes in the black neighborhoods.

Soon after the boycott began, city leaders met to discuss the demands.

They considered them outrageous. The only thing they agreed to do was to improve driver treatment of black passengers.

So the boycott went on. To get to their jobs, people shared cabs. Five people, paying 10 cents each, could pay the 45-cent minimum. Hoping to break the boycott, the city said the charge was 45 cents per person,

"No matter how many times they convict me," Martin said, the boycott would go on.

not per cab. How could a poor black afford so much?

Martin suggested they make up carpools and asked for volunteers. Soon 150 private cars were carrying workers to their jobs and back. Rich black women with Cadillacs were picking up poor blacks. In time, 300 private cars would help carry the blacks boycotting the buses.

As news of the boycott spread, letters of support and money came in. A man in Switzerland sent $500. A southern white woman wrote a letter to the newspaper saying the boycott was like Gandhi's movement in India. She became an outcast in the white community.

After the first meeting with city officials, the MIA sent a list of demands to the bus company president. They asked him to send someone to talk about the problems. The president said he would. But the man who arrived didn't contact the MIA. Instead, he met with city officials and became convinced the boycotters were wrong.

Meeting followed meeting, but no progress was made. The city officials were stalling. They were trying to divide the black community and turn them against Martin. They started rumors that the Kings drove expensive cars. They called Martin an outsider, trying to take over other black ministers' power.

It was the Christmas season. White businesses were suffering because fewer people came into the city to shop. Some businessmen tried to get city leaders to agree to the MIA demands. But they had no luck.

One day, Martin learned something disturbing from an out-of-town newsman. The next day's paper would have a story that the boycott had been settled. The news story would say city officials had reached agreement with three Montgomery black leaders. This wasn't true. It was just another attempt to break the boycott. If people believed it, they would start riding the buses again. Martin and other MIA members spent the night going from place to place telling people not to believe the story and to continue the boycott.

Angry that this plan didn't work, the mayor decided to get tough.

Carpool drivers were stopped by the police. They had to show their licenses and insurance papers. Riders waiting for their carpools were told they could be arrested for hitchhiking. Insurance companies refused to insure carpool drivers. Martin was arrested for driving 30 miles per hour in a 25-mile zone. When he was jailed, a huge crowd of blacks gathered outside. The police were worried. They let Rev. Abernathy pay bail to release Martin. Later, he was fined $10 for speeding.

By the end of January, the boycott was still going strong. Threatening phone calls began coming to Martin's home. One evening, Martin was away speaking at a church. About 9:30P.M., Coretta was sitting in the front room of her home with a woman friend. Suddenly, there was a loud thump on the porch and the squeal of a car picking up speed. Her friend jumped up.

"It sounds like someone hit the front of the house," Coretta said. "Let's move to the back." They ran toward the kitchen. Before they reached it, a loud explosion shook the house. They heard glass breaking and smelled smoke. Coretta ran to Yoki's room and grabbed her from the crib.

Martin was in the middle of a sermon when he noticed people whispering to each other. He asked what was wrong. When he learned, he said, "Someone has tried to bomb my house. I urge you all to go straight home. Straight home, hear me?"

He rushed home to find a big, angry crowd of friends outside his home. They began to sing "My County, 'Tis of thee," but the voices were roaring with rage. White reporters were afraid to go through the crowd. The mayor grabbed Martin's hand and said he was sorry. But it was the mayor's "get tough" policy that had brought on this kind of violence. Martin stepped to the front of his porch and held up his arms.

"I want you people to go home and put down your weapons," he said. "We must meet violence with non-

Martin telling friends not to use violence, after his home was bombed.

violence. He who lives by the sword shall perish by the sword. We must love our white brothers, no matter what they do to us . . . Remember, if I am stopped, this movement will not stop because God is with us . . ."

The boycott was hurting Montgomery. Lawyers dug into old state laws to find ways to stop it. It was illegal, they decided, for two or more people to block the operation of a business. The MIA leaders were arrested and Martin went to jail a second time. During the four day trial, witnesses told of the cruel bus drivers. One woman said her husband's foot was caught in the rear door of a bus. He was dragged many blocks because the driver wouldn't stop. Martin and other MIA members were sentenced to 386 days of hard labor in jail, or $500 and court costs. Friends posted money to free Martin until the case could be appealed.

Some six months after the boycott began, three federal judges declared by a two-to-one vote that bus segregation violated the Constitution. Montgomery officials were outraged. They appealed to the Supreme Court, the highest court in the land. Then, new violence broke out. E. D. Nixon's home was bombed. So were dozens of black churches. It was the work of the Ku Klux Klan, a secret society that used violence against blacks.

By October, ten months after the boycott started, the city asked the courts to rule on the legality of the carpool system. A hearing was set for November 13. Martin was worried. How could the boycott continue if the judge said carpools were illegal. As he waited for the judge's answer, a reporter ran up to him.

The Supreme Court had just ruled that bus segregation was illegal! Someone said, "God has spoken from Washington, D.C."

On December 21, 1956, 380 days after the boycott began, Martin, Abernathy, Nixon and several others went to catch the 6A.M. bus near Martin's home. Reporters and cameramen from all over the world covered the event. Martin climbed the front steps of the bus and dropped his dime in the box. The white driver said, "I believe you are Rev. King, aren't you?"

"Yes, I am," Martin said.

"We are glad to have you this morning," the driver said. Then, the first integrated bus in the history of the South rolled on down the street.

Bus boycotts now spread to other southern cities. Blacks all over the South began to feel they could

Three months after the bus boycott started, Martin and 92 other blacks were tried for disobeying segregation laws.

A years after the bus boycott began, the law was changed. Blacks could now sit where they pleased on buses.

"do something" to better their conditions.

The next month, Martin met with 60 black leaders and formed the Southern Christian Leadership Conference (SCLC). Their purpose was to make even greater gains for blacks. Martin was elected president.

One of the first acts of the SCLC was to hold a peaceful march on Washington, D.C. On May 17, 1957, nearly 30,000 black and white Americans from all over the country stood together before the Lincoln Memorial. There Martin set forth the next goal to seek—the right to vote.

Southern states made the test for registering to vote so hard that few blacks could pass. Because of this, hardly any blacks were able to vote. Now, Martin urged, "Give us the vote and we will write the proper laws on the books . . ."

Here, before the Lincoln Memorial in Washington,
Martin calls for laws to give black Americans equal
rights with white.

Martin spoke up again and again, urging the government to back civil rights. In 1958, he gave over 200 speeches. He told blacks to disobey laws that refused them rights white people enjoyed. He said they should go to jail peacefully.

Finally, in June, 1958, President Dwight D. Eisenhower met with Martin and other leaders. Eisenhower believed you could not "control the hearts of men with laws." Martin believed laws could at least "control how men act and behave." Martin wanted the President to give the Justice Department power to protect blacks trying to register to vote. He asked the President to refuse federal money to builders who wouldn't hire blacks as well as whites.

When Martin's first book, *Stride Toward Freedom*, came out, he autographed copies in New York. The book was about what happened in Montgomery. A black woman came up to him and asked, "Are you Dr. King?" When he said he was, she plunged a letter opener into his chest. Its point came so close to his heart that if he had sneezed, it would have killed him. The woman was declared insane.

Late in 1959, Martin stood before the members of his church. Much had happened in the five years he had been pastor there. Montgomery was known throughout the world. Martin had become a world leader. He wanted to do even more for his people. He would continue the struggle for civil rights from his father's church in Atlanta, he told them. "History has thrust something upon me which I cannot turn away," he said.

The service ended with the singing of "Blest Be the Tie That Binds."

Martin and Coretta celebrate publication of Martin's second book, Why We Can't Wait, *which deals with his experiences in the freedom movement.*

It was an old hymn always sung at times of parting. Martin, feeling the love of his friends, broke down and wept.

•

CHAPTER FIVE

SIT-INS, STAND-INS, KNEEL-INS FOR FREEDOM

Buses were now integrated by federal law. But segregation was still alive and well in the South. One day Martin met a white man on a flight to Atlanta. The man suggested they continue their talk at lunch in the airport restaurant. There Martin was told he would have to sit behind a curtain, away from his friend. He refused and left.

Soon after, two college students sat down at a bus station lunch counter. "We don't serve Negroes," the manager said. When the students left, they decided to start a boycott.

The next day, four students asked to be served at a Woolworth lunch counter. Whites were angry. They shouted names at them. The waitress wouldn't serve them. They returned day after day, saying they'd keep coming until they were served. That's how sit-ins started.

Within a month, students were sitting in at lunch counters, theaters, libraries, wherever blacks were not allowed. The sit-ins grew to include stand-ins, kneel-ins (at churches where blacks were denied membership) and mass marches. Police arrested students, hauling them off to jail roughly. Students did not resist. Martin met with 200 college students active in these new protests. He helped them form Student Non-Violent Coordinating Committee (SNCC).

One of the many times Martin was arrested.

The word was out to "get King."
He was a thorn in the side of the
white way of life. He wanted change.
White southerners wanted things as
they were. Alabama questioned his
state income tax and tried to charge
him with a false return. Georgia
grabbed him for driving without a
license. A few weeks later, he was
sentenced to four months in jail for
being in a sit-in. Still, progress was
being made, though slowly. Law
suits to gain voting rights for blacks
and to integrate schools were in-
creasing. Change was coming—
slowly.

Federal law made segregation in
buses illegal. But some buses, going
between states, were still segregated. So in May, 1961, the freedom
bus movement began.

It started on May 4. Thirteen students, white and black, boarded a
bus in Washington D.C. and headed

Coretta fixes a picnic basket for Martin, who has been in jail for ten days, while her children watch.

south. Wherever the bus stopped, they got out to sit at "whites only" lunch counters and to use "whites only" waiting rooms. When the bus reached Anniston, Alabama, a wild mob of whites met it. They set the bus on fire. The students barely escaped. They boarded another bus and headed for Birmingham. There a second mob attacked and beat them. The violence continued on other buses all through May. Finally, Attorney General Robert F. Kennedy ordered 400 U.S. marshals into Montgomery to keep order.

The situation was so bad that on May 21, Martin and a thousand people at the First Baptist Church became prisoners in the church. Outside, a huge mob of whites were throwing bottles and stones at the marshals and city police standing between them and the church. Inside, Martin and the congregation sang loudly "We Shall Overcome." It was the battle song of the freedom movement. Soldiers had to use tear gas to break up the crowd.

White churchmen began joining students in the freedom rides. Arrested, they went to jail with the blacks. The more violence the police used, the more people joined the movement. Finally, the cause was won. It became law that buses traveling between states must be integrated. Now, too, the law said, blacks could sit where they wished in bus or train waiting rooms and restaurants. Public facilities were for all to use. The freedom movement began with a bus boycott in one town. It brought about change throughout the South.

There was one city in the South as closed to change as a bank vault. It was Birmingham, Alabama. The Commissioner of Public Safety, Bull

Connor, was a tough, fat, white man. He vowed to keep all blacks in their place.

Martin decided Birmingham needed opening up. He began mass meetings in the black churches, and a few sit-ins. Then, on April 6, 1963, a march on City Hall was planned.

Three blocks from City Hall, a line of police blocked the marchers. When the marchers ignored the order to stop, the police began making arrests. The marchers did not resist. They sang freedom songs. Blacks who stood on the sidelines watching, were impressed. They, too, joined the Birmingham crusade for change.

On April 10, the city banned all demonstrations. Martin joined the protesters and was arrested. From jail he wrote what became the bible of the freedom movement. "There are two types of laws," he wrote.

"Just and unjust laws." What Hitler did in Germany was *legal,* yet what Hungarians fighting for freedom did was *illegal.* "We will reach the goal of freedom in Birmingham and all over the nation, because the goal of America is freedom."

In the next weeks, demonstrators marched and were arrested nearly every day. On May 2, almost 1,000 marchers were arrested. The next day, Bull Connor decided to end the problem once and for all. He ordered police to use high-powered water hoses, clubs and dogs against the marchers. That day hundreds of Birmingham's children were marching. They were singing, "Deep in my heart, I do believe that we shall overcome some day." These children, some as young as six years old, were knocked down, attacked by dogs or beaten.

Police dogs were used to break up marchers in Birmingham.

Birmingham firemen knock down demonstrators with high-powered water.

By May 7, Birmingham jails were bursting. Hurt by loss in business, white businessmen got together. They saw little choice. They agreed to the freedom movement demands. Lunch counters would be integrated. So would rest rooms, fitting rooms and drinking fountains. They would hire blacks and help get jailed marchers released. They would meet with black leaders to talk over other problems.

Birmingham, the city that had guarded the old ways so fiercely, had fallen to an army of nonviolence.

The Birmingham victory brought the government's full backing for the first time. President Kennedy announced, "One hundred years of delay have passed since President Lincoln freed the slaves, yet their grandsons are not fully free. Now the time has come for this nation to carry out its promise."

Peaceful protests moved to other southern cities. And Martin now planned a new demonstration.

To mark the 100th anniversary of the freeing of the slaves, he planned a large, peaceful march to the Lincoln Memorial in Washington. On August 28, 1963, 250,000 Americans, one in every four of them white, came to the nation's capitol from every state. All that long, hot day, they sat in the grass and sang freedom songs or listened to speeches. Finally, Martin spoke.

"I have a dream today," he said, ". . . a dream that my four little children will one day live in a nation where they will not be judged by the color of their skin, but by the content of their character." His deep voice carried over the sea of listening faces. "I have a dream," he continued, "that all God's children, black men and white men, Jews and

Martin leads march in Washington, D.C. in August, 1963.

Martin speaks on civil rights in Chicago at Soldier Field.

Gentiles . . . Protestants and Catholics, will be able to join hands . . ." Cheers rang out over the city. All those present wanted that same dream, and many wept.

Despite the gains in Birmingham and the peaceful protest in Washington, 1963 was marked by hate. Black leaders' homes were bombed. Medgar Evers, working for the NAACP, was murdered. A bomb, thrown into a Sunday school classroom, killed four young black children and injured many more. Then, in November, President John F. Kennedy was killed.

The new President, Lyndon B. Johnson, made a strong plea to Congress. Pass the civil rights bill for which Kennedy fought so hard, he urged. Perhaps its passage would heal some of the terrible wounds in America's civil rights war.

CHAPTER SIX

FREE AT LAST

As 1963 ended, Martin received the "Man of the Year" award from *Time* Magazine. He was called "a man of his people . . . for whom 1963 was perhaps the most important year in their history."

Early in the new year, Martin chose St. Augustine, Florida as the next site to protest. The city was the oldest in America and had been the center of the slave trade. More important, it was still 99 percent segregated!

With the Pope in Rome.

Peaceful protest marches were again met with violence. White gangs attacked marchers with clubs, chains, acid and bricks. Martin, Rev. Abernathy and other leaders were jailed under Florida's "unwanted guest law." Martin, the villain, spent two days in jail before being released on bail. He immediately went to Yale University. There, before 10,000 cheering people, he became a "hero." He was awarded an honorary degree for refusing to use violence. The next day he was back in Florida, again a villain.

On July 2, 1964, Congress passed the Civil Rights Bill, the one Kennedy had asked for before he was killed. It called for desegregation of all public places. Refusing jobs or votes just because of a person's color became illegal. The law was clear. Making people obey it was another matter.

That fall, after a trip to West Berlin as a guest of its mayor and a visit with the Pope, Martin received some marvelous news. He learned he would be given the Nobel Peace Prize in Oslo, Norway. The award is given to the person judged to have done the most to contribute to peace and understanding throughout the world. Martin was the third black and the youngest person ever to be so honored.

On December 10, 1964, Martin accepted the award in the name of the civil rights movement. In the audience, beaming and proud, were Martin's parents, Coretta and the children—Yoki, Martin, III, Dexter and Bernice. The medal and gold watch Martin would keep. But the cash award of $56,400 would be donated to the freedom movement.

Soon after the trip to Oslo, Martin went to Selma, Alabama. In Selma,

Martin's father, mother, wife and sister on the way to the Nobel Peace Prize ceremony.

After receiving the 1964 Nobel Peace Prize in Oslo, Norway.

only two percent of the blacks of voting age had been allowed to register, even though the law said it was illegal to keep them from registering. He wanted to bring this fact before the American public and the government. The vote was a weapon. With it, blacks could elect people who would fight for their rights.

Again, as in other cities where marchers protested, arrests were made and jails began to fill. Martin was in jail again; in his lifetime he was in prison 30 times. "There are more Negroes in jail with me," he said, "than there are on the voting rolls."

The world was especially interested in news from Selma. After all, the Nobel Peace Prize winner was there. Then, on February 18, 1965, one of the marchers was shot. He died eight days later. Martin called for a mass march from Selma to Montgomery. Jimmie Lee Jackson's death must not be in vain.

Governor George Wallace forbade the march, but the protesters ignored his order. The march began peacefully, with about 550 blacks and whites. They walked through Selma and across the Edmund Pettus Bridge. There, at the other end of the bridge, were state police, the sheriff and over a hundred men. They were armed with guns, clubs and tear gas. "Stop!" the marchers were told. They stopped. "Break it up and go back!" When they refused, they were struck by bullwhips, knocked under horses' hooves, chased and hit with clubs, and fired on with tear gas. By the end of the day, 17 people were in hospitals.

This brutal treatment of the protesters made many more come to Selma to join the marchers. Among

Marching for voting rights from Selma to Montgomery, 54 miles away.

them were many white ministers.
Then, Rev. James Reeb of Boston, a
white minister, was attacked by a
white mob and died. His death
aroused even more anger against the
white mobs. President Johnson con-
demned the violence. He sent a new
bill to Congress making illegal all
methods used to deny people the
right to vote.

On March 21, the Selma to Montgomery march began with the pro-
tection of federal marshals. Martin
and Coretta and other well-known
black leaders led it off. They sang
"We Shall Overcome." At the end of
the march, Martin outlined more
goals. "Let us march on segregated
schools, on poverty, on the ballot
boxes . . ." Always, he repeated, *protest without violence!*

In August, 1965, the Selma protest paid off. A voting rights bill was
passed into law. No longer could

men and women be kept from voting just because they were black.

In the next year, Martin planned ways to bring about more civil rights. The movement had started in 1955 with Rosa Parks' refusal to give up her seat to a white man. Now, over ten years later, Martin's efforts and those of other leaders had brought about many changes. Black people had gained a new sense of pride in being part of the struggle. They were beginning to believe they could play an equal role in America's destiny.

In late 1966, Martin took a stand on the Vietnam war. The war was not popular with many Americans. It was costly in loss of life as well as in dollars. Martin accused the government of putting the war before the problems of the people at home. That money should be put into improving education, in housing for the poor and in jobs and training for people out of work.

Many of his supporters turned against him. At that time, it was an unpopular stand to take on the war. Also, Black Power was on the rise. Militant blacks—men and women who found nonviolence too slow in bringing change—were gaining followers. Rioters tore their neighborhoods apart in the summer of 1967. They burned stores and stole what they couldn't afford to buy. They wanted what other Americans had —jobs, cars, nice homes. And they wanted it Now!

Martin opposed the violence, but he understood it. He said riots were "the language of the unheard." He said "revolts came from revolting conditions." Put more money into helping the poor, he begged the government.

The first months of 1968 saw Martin planning a big "Poor People's March." The poor would go to Washington to let their needs be known. He wanted the government to assure a minimum yearly income for each family.

But before the Poor People's March, he had to help lead a protest in Memphis. There garbage workers were asking for better conditions and higher pay. On April 3, 1968, Martin, Rev. Abernathy and others in their group checked into a motel in Memphis.

Martin's personal safety had always been a worry. But in recent months, he seemed especially aware of danger. He had developed a habit of "looking behind him suddenly, and without reason," a friend said.

On the evening of April 4, he was in a very good mood. He was looking forward to joining friends for a dinner of his favorite soul food. He came

Martin planned a poor people's march on Washington before he was killed.

out of his motel room and leaned over the balcony. He was waiting for Rev. Abernathy. At 6:40P.M., as he chatted with friends on the stairs and in the parking lot below, there was a single loud crack. Martin fell. He had been hit by an assassin's bullet. Later, James Earl Ray, an ex-convict, was accused and convicted of the crime. He was sent to jail for life.

Martin, on the motel balcony, the day before he was shot.

Only the day before, Martin had said, "Like anybody, I would like to live a long life. But I'm not concerned about that now. I just want to do God's will. And he's allowed me to go up to the mountain. And I've looked over, and I've seen the promised land. I may not get there with you, but I want you to know tonight that we as people will get to the promised land."

Martin Luther King, Jr. had led the civil rights fight. His efforts had brought over $20 million to the cause. Yet, on the day he died, he left his family only $5,000 in cash and a small life insurance policy. Friends would contribute to a fund to support his widow and children.

On April 9, 1968, with the flag flying at half-mast, Martin Luther King, Jr. was laid to rest. A service was held at the Ebenezer Baptist Church in Atlanta. Then the casket

Coretta comforts Bernice during funeral services.

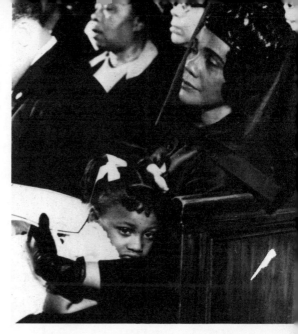

A mule cart carries Dr. Martin Luther King, Jr.'s casket through Atlanta.

was loaded on a farm wagon drawn by two mules. A throng of 150,000 people, black and white, judges, Congressmen, men and women from every walk of life, followed it. Many wept.

Martin Luther King, Jr., the man whose dream had only just begun, was dead. On his gravestone were carved these words from an old slave song: "Free at Last. Free at Last. Thank God Almighty, I'm Free at Last."